Tractors

BY HAL ROGERS

The Child's World

Published by The Child's World®
1980 Lookout Drive • Mankato, MN 56003-1705
800-599-READ • www.childsworld.com

Acknowledgments
The Child's World®: Mary Berendes, Publishing Director
The Design Lab: Design
Jody Jensen Shaffer; Editing
Pamela J. Mitsakos: Photo Research

Photos
Chukov /Shutterstock.com: 20; Dmitry Kalinovsky/
iStock.com: 16; Inger Anne Hulbækdal/iStock.com:
12; jennyt/Shutterstock.com: 19; Kali Nine LLC/
iStock.com: 7; Luis Louro/iStock.com: 4; Photobac/
Shutterstock.com: cover, 1; smereka/Shutterstock.com:
8, 15; vladimir salman/Shutterstock.com: 9

ISBN 9781623239718
LCCN 2013947257

Printed in the United States of America
Mankato, MN
November, 2013
PA02190

Contents

Tractors come in all sizes and colors.

What are tractors?

Tractors are powerful vehicles
They might not move fast. But
they are built to do hard work.
They can pull or push very
heavy loads. Many tractors are
used on farms. But tractors do
other jobs, too!

What parts do tractors have?

The driver uses **controls** to run the tractor. On many tractors, the driver sits in a **cab**. Tractors sometimes tip over. The cab keeps the driver safe. Other tractors have an outside seat. A seat belt and roll bar keep the driver safe.

The driver steers with a steering wheel, just like a car.

This tractor does not have a cab. The driver sits in the seat.

engine

Tractors do heavy work. They need a big **engine** to provide power. The engine's power moves the tractor. It can run other tools and machines, too.

What are tractors used for?

Different kinds of tractors do different jobs. Farm tractors often pull other machines. They pull **plows** to get fields ready for planting. They pull machines that plant seeds or pick crops. They do other farm work, too.

This farm tractor
is being used
to plow a field.

Lawn tractors can be loud. Many owners wear ear protection.

Lots of people have small lawn or garden tractors. These tractors are good for mowing grass. They help with other yard work, too.

Sometimes tractors have a big **blade** on the front. The blade can easily push dirt, rocks, or snow. Bulldozers are tractors with blades. Bulldozers also have **crawler tracks** instead of wheels. Crawler tracks move well on bumpy ground or soft dirt.

blade

crawler tracks

Loaders can be used for many different jobs.

Loaders are tractors with a bucket on the front. The bucket picks things up. Loaders work in all kinds of places. They move rock and dirt. They move trash at city dumps. They even move snow.

Diggers are tractors with a **backhoe**. The backhoe has a long arm. The arm has a bucket on the end. The backhoe digs and scoops dirt and rocks.

Diggers can scoop heavy piles of dirt and rocks.

Plowing is just one important job that tractors can do!

Are tractors important?

Tractors are used all over the world. They pull heavy machines. They plow fields. They push dirt and snow. They dig holes. They help people build things. Tractors are very important!

GLOSSARY

backhoe (BAK-ho) A backhoe is a digging scoop on a long arm.

blade (BLAYD) A blade is a part that is broad, flat, and usually thin. The blade on a tractor pushes things.

cab (KAB) A machine's cab is the area where the driver sits.

controls (kun-TROHLZ) Controls are parts that people use to run a machine.

crawler tracks (KRAWL-ur TRAKS) Crawler tracks are metal belts that some machines use for moving.

engine (EN-jun) An engine is a machine that makes something move.

plows (PLOWZ) Plows are tools that turn soil and break it up before it is planted.

vehicles (VEE-uh-kulz) Vehicles are things for carrying people or goods.

BOOKS

Bingham, Caroline. *Tractor*. New York: DK Publishing, 2004.

Coppendale, Jean. *Tractors and Farm Vehicles.* Richmond Hill, ON: Firefly Books, 2010.

Nelson, Kristin L. *Farm Tractors*. Minneapolis, MN: Lerner Publications, 2003.

Young, Caroline. *Tractors*. London: Usborne Publishing, 2003.

WEB SITES

Visit our Web site for lots of links about tractors:
childsworld.com/links

Note to parents, teachers, and librarians: We routinely check our Web links to make sure they're safe, active sites—so encourage your readers to check them out!

INDEX

ABOUT THE AUTHOR

Hal Rogers has written over a dozen books on machines and trucks. A longtime resident of Colorado, Hal currently lives in Denver, along with his family, a fuzzy cat named Simon, and a lovable dog named Sebastian.